NOVEMBER'S VICTIM

NOVEMBER'S VICTIM

•

A COLLECTION OF POEMS
QUOTES AND ILLUSTRATIONS

•

JOE LOVETT

LARKSPUR BOOKS

Joe Lovett

November's Victim

A Collection of Poems Quotes and Illustrations

Library of Congress Cataloging-in-Publication Data
Lovett, Joe
    November's Victim
    A Collection of Poems Quotes and Illustrations

ISBN-13: 978-0615444888
ISBN-10: 0615444881

Library of Congress Control Number: 2011901742

Designed by Joe Lovett

Printed and bound in the United States of America.

10 9 8 7 6 5 4 3 2 1

for my lovely daughter

Belzora

Contents

POEMS

ILLUSTRATIONS

QUOTES

November's Victim

And then came the victim,
cold rain falls hitting a face in dark mischief
changing patterns different during day than before–
A memory of the seventh,
and the careless chatter of adolescence,
It must be November.

Death of the Insane

It came from a far away place in the mind
with this confusion they call a solution,
A man with golden vision pushed away petty humor,
Is it just senseless paranoia?
Or, the stuff dreams are made of?
Only the insane perish before their time–
He will give the guidance that you seek,
cluttering the brain with this task
losing time spent as well as the mind,
so you run from the pain
as more than one voice reams the ear of sanity.

———————●———————

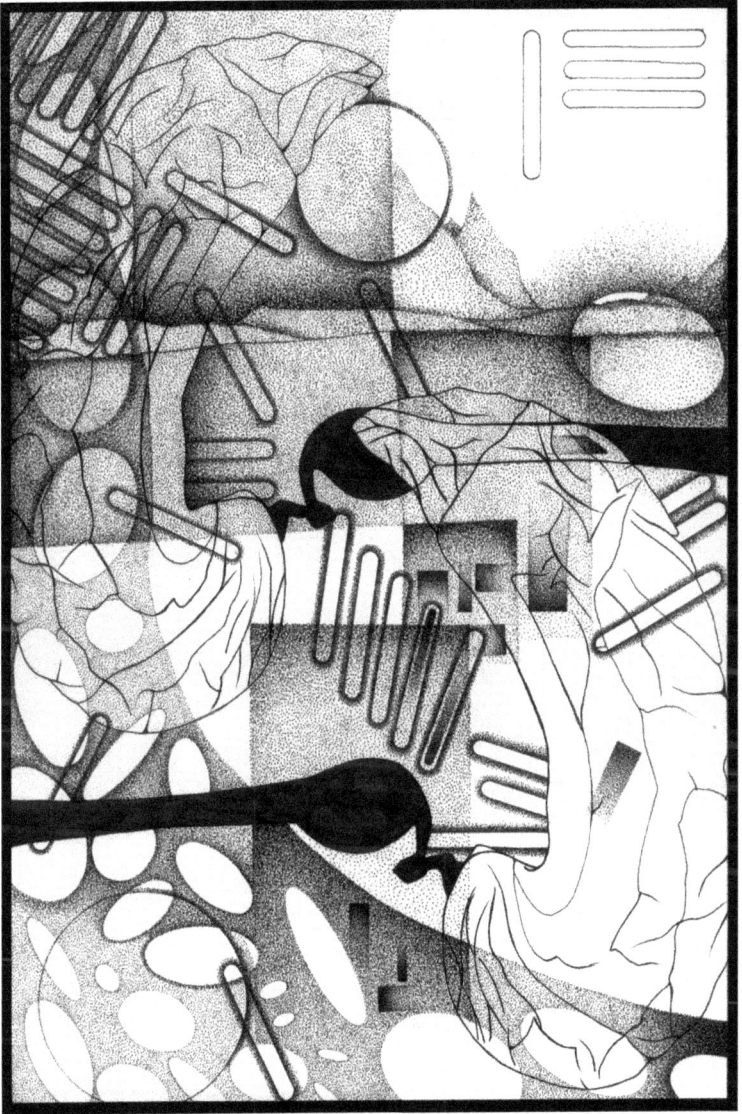

Death of the Insane

I would rather exist within anonymous accomplishment, than excel within the public accolades of mediocracy.

———————●———————

The Storm

I smell the storm, a twist of minds cohorting
with candles in the sky,
The orgasm wet and long leaving the
scent of her silent bliss,
Her loins clap together with his–
The aroma of relief and relaxation,
One day with the illusion of two.

Movies on the Moon

And everyone knows how to do it,
How to die–
But not knowing how to face it,
A legitimate reason driving down the road
projecting movies on the moon,
scratching maggots from our hair.

————————●————————

Painful Posture

Have you ever felt like putting one in?
Bringing an end so the next one can begin,
How many voices must be heard?
Are they just mimicking the painful posture
in which we sit?
Today's emotions confuse us all
and the reverence of loss adds to it.

————————●————————

Hot Brown Eyes

My dream should first of all be very tiny and red,
She must be polite,
A profile like horny toads,
If there's any trouble going to sleep
you probably have a sexy mind, so
you must first drink a cup of
hot brown eyes.

———————•———————

Shades from the butterfly,
Flap your wings stirring clouds and wind–
Let us play in your sanctum.

———————•———————

Rain

Do you remember the short moment?
The lifetime we've spent,
Passion caressed the soul
concern eased the pain,
Your sky is mine,
make me smile in quiet night,
Life drops like rain.

Not unlike the wind in my hair,
Caressing my thoughts,
you belong there.

Glabrous and Sinister

The isolation deafened the soul with impotent output,
Potential is dead–
Mediocre motions yawn with lazy creation,
There he is glabrous and sinister,
The assassin was witnessed–
Or, was it a state of non being?
An intoxicating haze blistered their surroundings
like an informal invitation.

———————•———————

Glabrous and Sinister

Place

Combat, the next move nervous and pure
with voice newborn,
A place fell to the plan–
Tailor made hand me downs arrive
even lower now with baited breath,
craving the full strain.

Her

Could that have been her he asked,
A memory flew by and began to fade
carving history from his, the divine lover
left behind false faces, he proceeded as planned.

Tall Walls

Stubborn guest never to budge,
eyes lash the dead smile,
shall we read the faded reflections
without cohersion or reward,
Tall walls of useful instrument
unable to bear growth's dull edge.

Madmen

Barking thunderous dog stream
awakened by phone chants–
Oh, no one's there,
Strangers follow us with lust or leer
choking on eyes of society,
Tongues, and lords,
Madmen won't disagree.

———————•———————

The Harvest

Nature's way, infinite, existing,
We destroy soil, scorched,
Cleared for paved plots,
Will we then be a thing of mystery,
and nothing more?
Harvest our decline–
Regret's day will come to enjoy us all.

The Trip

Can't stand the silence
listening to my thoughts,
Will this one be the last?
The journey from which there is no return–
Slam the door,
Shadows dwell of footsteps at the entrance.

Spawns

A song played,
Beauty unlocked and perceived,
The hiss of talk radio followed,
Our spawns were that of the chameleon.

Something in Common

The public transported us,
A death scene at first glance,
Life lost, covered with a sheet
broken window near top floor,
Second glance we've arrived,
Whispers danced from the crowd,
Third glance suicide.

———————●———————

Insincerity

Seeing through the vows of insincerity
the glass ring shattered in her hand
cutting love veins that hurt so good,
The same one-nighter that shattered
the ring also shattered her soul,
The flame that once burned,
grew, grew transparent,
A darkened room cast shadows of naked
silhouettes seeing through what never was.

———————•———————

Staggered Strength

She called my daily routine, our distant days,
Absence answered all that it could,
Love for us has staggered strength
placed here for good or bad,
Memory's moment has captured flesh,
Loan me the morning screen–
Reception remains unclear on the floor.

The answers fell–
After the truth was told,
Once again allowed to be free.

———————●———————

The Left Step

Tick tock,
Tick tock,
Let me annoy you with that sound,
Tick tock,
Tick tock
No escape and then the fade–
Time piece–
Right hand–
The left step growing
louder same as above,
Sudden silence reached.

———————•———————

Those that try to deny your capabilities, have taken the first step to recognizing their own inadequacies, and for that they should be commended.

———————●———————

Porcelain

Speed up the pace pass,
Both ways capture thorough-breds,
Ownership howls like nighttime,
Clothes smell sour,
Wadded–
Wet–
Scrubbing our porcelain stains from waste,
Taped shows turn slow,
Necks stiffen the morning mood.

———•———

Comedy and Tragedy

Hate–
Is this what you call a home?
uprooted from the birthright,
Greed–
The common friend of apocalypse,
Inventor of demise,
Love–
A day of rest–
The event reared an unplanned approach
emotion grew with discriminating ease,
Death–
Shedding hopeful symbols,
bringing us wisdom beyond belief.

————————●————————

Parking lots for tow trucks,
The garbage comes on Wednesday,
Walkway wet with red paint in midday,
Holiday's pay unable to resume set schedules,
Time clocks shallow with reprimand,
Office whispers control.

Though we strive for perfection, our arrogance
allows us to fail in the face of wisdom.

———————●———————

Strange Recipe

Echoes shine from the top,
Our trapped hands open corner stores
abundant with chemical remedies,
Posted and vulnerable we must offend,
Old photos told only small parts–
A porch odd and familiar,
The standard of strange recipe.

———•———

Grace gave the gift,
Morning song birds have sung,
I awake with language.

Day of the Child

He scratched the surface of possibility,
Has the blood lust been graduated?
No return in sight to the drab existence
of what seems to have been only yesterday,
The itch gives want for open infection,
Leather becomes the skin–
The growth of a man making
way for playful imagination,
Like the day of the child.

Do not take unless supervised,
Constipated rectangles distract consuming
motorists in the slow lane,
Turn signals love gas pains and underpants.

Hours in Time

Can we speak with hours in time,
At one point seems will never return–
Emotions–
So new.

Old Textures

Will it work, not knowing?
More time–
But inside, you know what I mean,
Take away old textures,
But please do not enter.

———————•———————

Day of Occupance

One hundred days of occupance
she created stories of rape,
I love your mind without permission,
The pores from my face create city soot stench,
Once again old friend,
once again numbers dance,
The sweat pillow has awakened me
from romance.

Commodity

Commodity for intercourse faded another face,
common only to those who know of nothing else,
Cheap suits run the show–
Will she wait for the call.

A King's Madness

These are the hours of a king's madness,
Her next meal will be the last as
decoration adorns humiliation,
The memory of our servants will be broken,
A jester sang the song of secrets.

A Dark Time

Our guardian grew curious,
Contacted by questions that began during a dark time,
Grant me one wish–
A season smooth with boxes folded,
Stored behind scrap piles.

Trees form mountains
Planting green pictures of homesick,
A wind whispers.

Thumb of Promiscuity

Sins caressed nightmares,
Lullabies eased the pain–
On this night changes occur, catching
rain drops on the thumb of promiscuity,
For the dreams of a mother I send this message–
I've found happiness in death,
finally alone but altogether.

———————●———————

Toxicity's enticement pulses through the accumbens
nucleus with memories of high levels and stimulants.

Birth of New Nations

The boyish presence, a fearful hatred of justice,
Twenty past the hour, is death humoring the man?
Put in this position by the weak and unfortunate,
Failure hung by a thread on what life used to be,
These are the feelings that present
the troubled minds that lie ahead,
News at five another homicide–
News at eleven another suicide–
Not just the plan but the actions that they take,
The birth of new nations
destroying ancient wisdom,
Injustice has been done.

A private smile,
A shy embrace,
Let's enjoy late night chastity snacks,
Silent screens flicker.

Bruised

Hear me without words or tone,
Speak for me–
Merge with my soul,
Learn me,
Learn you,
How odd, no sign of struggle, although
vigorous movement was evident,
Odd indeed–
An empty room,
Still–
Quiet.

There comes a time when academia's
influence will become worn and thin,
therefore it is now up to our own queries,
to stopple the resonant voices of clogged ears.

———————●———————

Failed

A dream saw the past
Future events told stories of such
When all that's left,
A memory?
Paradox–
Complexity's demise,
A time when movement quickened,
everything stood still–
Laughter has failed us.

Celebration

The oval office of destruction
did what needed to be done,
Wasting many lives for the sake of who's freedom?
Overgrown embryo of life emerging–
Running rampant through the pockets of celebration.

———————●———————

Allowing others to dictate your
self worth is an idolatrous act,
and should be vehemently challenged.

———————•———————

Sarah

Sad that day,
A friend set free,
Released from selfish pain,
Fixed and dilated before an
audience of silent reaction,
Watch over me.

Eight Hour Day

Fashioned by fascination with studious
contempt now entrenched on the fields,
Mental wars,
Battles of the flesh–
Social puppets on the strings of advertisement,
And to think–
That's just the end of an eight hour day.

————————●————————

Sometimes you must go past the point of no return to reach the destination that suites ones needs in order to capture a vision of the future, unmarred by static interference.

———————●———————

The Stranger

Wanting–
The youth so soft and beautiful,
In this void relationships grow
with insatiable habit,
Change and again with change
like an indecisive prostitute,
Long closet walls of sinful garment
startled by the stranger who
walked silently up the stairs.

The Wise Way

Patterns mute with despair,
Age will continue to teach the wise way,
Barriers fall, now lighter than air,
Still wondering who I am,
Where are the rest of my friends?
Here we are,
Where?
Right here inside of you.

Mind Drift

Few are in the heart,
Time is in the now, flowing mind drift,
Man–
Woman–
Child–
Take a breath for the rest of your life.

One of the hardest obstacles to overcome as
an independent thinker has been to detach
myself from peer influence.

Playground

Games in the short space,
Playgrounds seem to just get by,
Sounds disturb, shrill yet innocent,
So we must remember–
Not yet full grown with pitch,
The gain of knowledge never wanting to rest,
Every new adventure full.

———————●———————

Table Scraps

Piano bars scatter to meet the next order on demand,
Wealth's stemware full,
Golden–
Tailored and amber,
Eyes caught by dual perceptions, high or low,
Bus tubs trap table scraps,
Dirty dishes.

Naked Fear

Soldier to many, a battalion of one stands alone,
Confusion–
The naked fear of destiny tempting the body,
Shadows flow like parts of a dream,
hard to remember to strange to forget,
The truth told lies from the past,
blinding false images of life.

———————●———————

Political correctness will destroy our capability
of self expression.

———————•———————

Residue

Residue,
Is that what's left for you and me?
Let us taste, and decide,
A strange flavor–
A strange act–
Was it sweet or sour?
Strange indeed.

Some things are best left unsaid, especially in a room full of opinionated people.

———————●———————

Abstract Action

Your train of thought has brought you here,
This tedious addiction of lucrative
positioning breeds great fear,
Sighs of discontent remind us of the
despair in which we dwell,
Each day uncertain–
The quiet relief of abstract action
will remain until the last.

The Secret

My heart overflows with the secret,
No one to share my thoughts,
Surrounded–
Yet still alone,
Sinking deep and fast
this depression becomes a home-
Growing bitter,
Go back into the shell,
My heart overflows with the secret,
As I turn there's no one to tell.

Halls

Invade my chapter of temporary presence,
Regard it with no respect–
Numbered halls jailed with the schedule of freedom,
Easy access becomes a greater mystery
and challenges everyone involved,
Repeat the words after me,
Jobs love sweet vapors drifting from the mind's idea,
Narrow with brief escape,
Weakened–
Destroyed–
Forgotten.

My work is transcendental, so when asked about the inspiration of a piece, my response is, somewhere between here and there.

———————●———————

Shape

We consume ink, pulp,
Eyes bulge–
Conversation's shape shall quickly form now–
Outside smiles polite appearance no longer in,
The blows become abrupt, strong and sudden–
Words of innocence never again to speak it's soft voice.

———————●———————

Shape

What one finds humorous others
may find ill-mannered,
so do not presume that your
humorist nature is universal.

Ghetto Gardens

Slumlords and ghetto gardens drooling for the toys
of the rich, a poor pawn lost in the shallow grave
of society's chess game,
Given a higher outlook–
They rejoice and feed the children,
The sickness grows peaks of pleasure and pain
crying for enlightenment in the name of a dollar,
The dead shall rise again.

———————●———————

My Question

Why do we use the names we've created?
Why do we use the names that are hated?
Turmoil sitting in it's bliss–
A struggle for harmony so easy to
use and abuse yet so hard to find,
Is this the meaning?
Self preserving thoughts causing havoc on mankind,
Our third generation of failure,
Will the next one be the same?
The question is asked.

Comprehending the application of one thing, invites infinite possibilities.

———————●———————

Flower of Souls

The ancient tides caressed by new moons,
Are there any ears listening?
Or, just the worthless words of friendly gesture
waking to an existence,
The sweet presence of nectar–
Maturing ideas of the inner self,
growing like a flower of the soul.

Flower of Souls

The sound of sewer rats
rummaging the cement floors,
Prisons,
Jails,
Sniffing through garbage pails.

Feud's birth, quiet with no trace,
Disguise the pains of temporary risk
and volume's sterile path,
Quick hands rationed slowly
discipline shall remain,
The applicant almost complete to
chore without complaint,
Dissolve the talk of crowded days
to board the quiet train.

The Loss

Zip zip zoom scurry across your floor of mazes,
Being swept up in the dust combustion,
pulling into the stall of economy,
Find your freedom to create,
Take time to punch in late,
Listen to the silence of her majesty's bliss,
feel the wetness of her morning mist.

———————●———————

From a Son

Love is a word to express deep feeling,
Joy comes to mind for a mother,
Like no other–
Such as mine.

Blind Route

Seeker of thoughts perhaps hidden
behind thin layers of milky tissue
and freeways of blind route,
Newcomers distract various stops
directed by daily merchants that
combust with no promise–
Bathe our scoured skin, raw and tender
uneven from the ground up,
Product of poor gated labors deny exit,
Nutrition's window opened, starved–
Awaiting energy's dose.

Stretch the Strangle Hold

Stretch the strangle hold,
March with young and old,
Scold my third rough sketch,
Life's time takes its toll,
Sized and sure to fit,
Fit for no one's mold,
Birth's result is our first test,
Stretch the strangle hold–
Stretch the strangle hold–
Our young blush soft, shared by first kiss,
Thoughts they fade ignored and dismissed.

Window of Silence

The last hand of mercy washed away access,
Entombed by a cocoon of four walls,
the benevolent song plays with no
room for society in the vast vision of one,
Glistening warmth cast from the
leaves, which fall from the tree of solitude–
Sarcastic melody communicating through
the window of silence,
A friend for the moment is made.

Stay Alert Stay Alive

These are the days that recess in painful memory,
A separate story told by the aging masses,
shadowed, torn by war and deception,
In the midst of the phenomenon,
A day started–
A life soon to begin, and many more to be lost,
In a land known as Vietnam.

———————●———————

Tony's Pedestrian

Tony's pedestrian shared innocence
similar and harsh,
Formed from foreign occurrence
as laughter enjoyed itself without regret,
New personality must allow pause for
the awkward moment colors hold,
Amazement set–
Freed by the course–
Ooooooh–
I'd like that rewound with exact
order facing habit's birth,
Mental days of absent labor find my excuse,
Rooms of rest often share frowns of future use.

Tony's Pedestrian

Self expression is a necessary fabric of life, without it, our identities would remain anonymous.

———————●———————

A calming came about, and the
braided scent fell upon us,
Harmony crisp with expertise
being directed by one million dictations,
Chasing the tail of confusion.

The importance of dreams is more than an occurrence
of possibilities, but the passing of impotent imagery.

———————•———————

Sex, Vision, Blues

A new dwelling replaces the old,
Another replaced the new with surroundings
drowning out painful voices with sexy rhythm,
and joyous visions.

———●———

Generations

Will the tools we use today also be named ancient?
Or, will there be no one left to know?
The urban children's plight–
The ignorance of racist generations–
Or, will the visions of the past destroy
what has not yet been done?
What have the mothers and fathers left
for their children? Another generation
of hopelessness and despair?
A time of change writes new beginnings–
Death gave birth to the mother of extinction
and the wrath of a new virus.

Shadows gave knowledge of movement,
The enemy of our people are swift,
They come to us during the rains,
Ambush is their goal–
Warfare is certain.

Would you name the time
between two places an end or a start?
What should I wear to the party?
Maybe the costume of a sick dream–
She showed us her cock and
her womanhood amazed us all,
Science dissected her tools,
and made its own assessment.

———————●———————

The Individual

Wake up to the criticism of my desire,
Wake up to the criticism of my beliefs, the
reality of my pain, the insanity of your grief,
In your delusions you say you're the one I want
bearing the children of deceit,
The question waiting for response,
The destruction of man we will meet,
Unsuccessful dominance of the ones you fear
in this nation of a louder voice,
Not everyone can be you nor can they be me,
But there should always be this freedom we call choice.

———————●———————

The Funeral

He cried not necessarily for the man he never knew,
but for the family he loves,
as he sees and feels their pain,
The tall bulky man reduced to
emotional turmoil hiding the pain,
his face frozen with grief,
The women, this wicked black widow
of greed and infidelity,
The brothers, the sons, the tribe–
A family of one coming together
for the man's last day.

Counting Cups

The fool played the role of the scholar,
Seriousness followed almost to the point of laughter,
Well read–
Well kept–
Bred for what opposition,
Counting cups,
Sorting silverware.

———————●———————

When living becomes so loud,
We induce ourselves,
We seduce ourselves,
We reduce ourselves,
Swim the tides, dance with my love,
Love me,
Love me,
Let me go.

————————•————————

Subconscious Criminal

Something so old seems so new,
a person's face like an aging friendship,
shell of emptiness, mist of life deciding,
laughter in the background–
Who are you they think, a
sheltered thought of self image,
Mind lingering deception, life threatening
uncontrollable doubts, hanging from a string
for a subconscious criminal.

———————•———————

Standing Alone

Sometimes I feel like I'm the only one,
like I'm just wasting my time,
Though it's been done before, I share the feeling now,
of fear, hopelessness, anger, and sorrow,
Sometimes I feel like I'm the only one,
but I keep my head up, longing for mental
success to fight for whats right,
I may not see your god,
but I feel peace in my heart,
I may not see your devil
but I feel evil and hate,
Sometimes I feel like I'm the only one,
in this twisted fight for unity,
But I know the past, and now know, that I'm not alone.

————•————

Short Sitters

A voice has been chosen in the area of
hard reform, here we travel with the short sitters,
Boring excitement brings us the counter of days,
shall we rest in the arms of solitude and
the possibility of arrest,
Everyday occurrence but so little we speak,
Showing the heart of dreams,
Sacred are the walls of reclusion.

———————●———————

I have received my transcendental package in the mail, now all that's left, is to turn down the sheets.

———————•———————

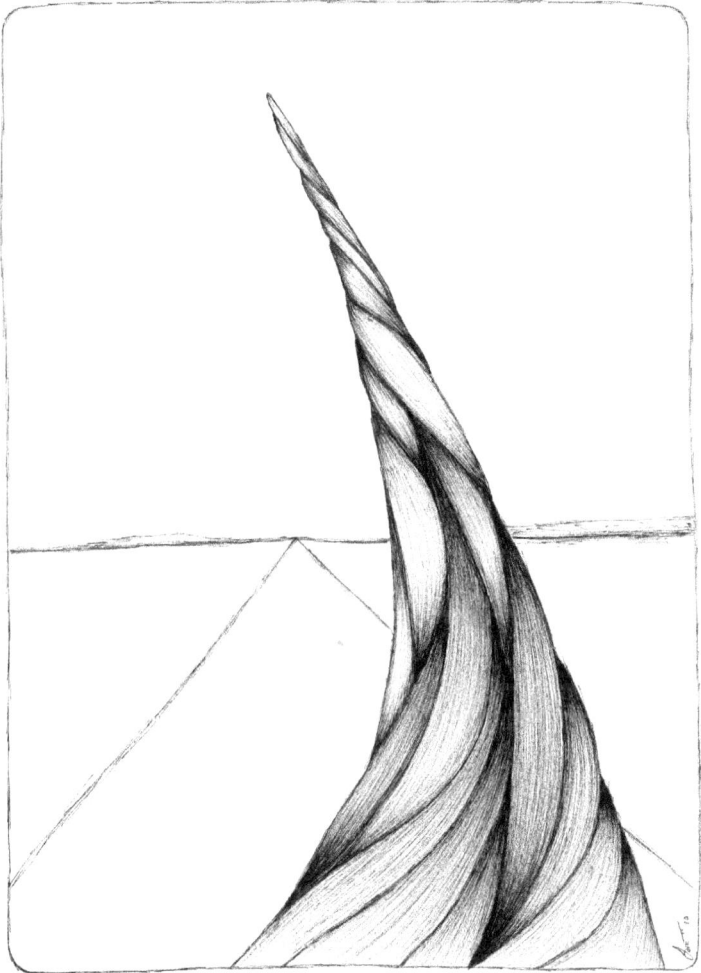

Obstacle

Myth

Let's experiment with this old formula, will it
open more paths or tear them down with brilliance,
Scared of sacred myth stacked high on a night
of triumph, forever leaving the riches behind,
All of us can question–
Doubt–
In this trance mystery, the time has not come for us
to meet the elders and their ancient power of story.

————————•————————

Consumed

Hard for me to see as I open my
eyes at the start of my day,
As I lift my head–
I wake from the only peace I feel,
Nothing like it,
Consumed by the menial way.

Red 97

Why plant the seed?
Game of guilt featuring what is soon to be,
Shoes of warm women purchase the morning–
An aging face obtained knowledge of demise
as new skin grows for old flesh,
Hands bronze with age–
Hardship.

———————●———————

Red 97

If you expect your roads to not have obstacles, then you will never prepare yourself for alternative routes.

Stray

Stray into my numb swollen fingers
and tell the stories they can tell,
The second shift is on the prowl
for wealth of grief, or wealth itself,
The heavy things are better,
No memories,
Just dreams.

———————●———————

Morning Conversation

Piracy has not been forgotten,
amassed is our fixation with the
golden trinkets and higher ranks,
What does it all mean?
Oh, nothing,
Just a thought of a talk show,
Would you like a cup of coffee?
No thank you, I never touch the stuff.

As life gets simpler, the truly important things become more evident.

Fine Wine

A fly on the wall said that things will be fine
so lets attack the political cancer,
Your vote counts,
All tallied up in the waste of life's policy–
I request asylum from your point of view,
Give me refuge–
Thank you little fly it's all clear now,
it's all fine wine– big business and realities
collide, pay the box to pray and confide–
A fly on the wall said everything must be fine wine,
so take the grapes to our office and thank us.

Again I Mourn

Mourning the loss before it is,
So let us share the last bath on
a ride to who knows where amidst
this man made tragedy,
Love is never ending,
And forever the end.

Sometimes its best to observe quietly, and enjoy the moment without an all knowing conversationalist.

———————●———————

Seventy

Garden stones are there for the taking,
Burning flames contract dust from the sky,
Here I am,
Here we are,
Both strange but who is stranger?
Here I am,
Here we are,
What is life's range?
What is, Life's range?
What is life's range.

The work itself is the most rewarding of all payments, any monetary gain is a social formality strictly for the portrayal of success.

————————●————————

Eyes of Discontent

Glaring,
Chasing,
Chastising my humanity,
The very thought of my existence–
Here I am among you–
Born dead,
Born silent,
Born–
Among you.

Nobody

Nobody is that quiet walk down the road,
When the hit of a familiar scent reminds you,
A time long gone, and still longing,
A reminder, not of loneliness,
but the harsh surroundings–
To be seen, and not known,
To make jest, and not be seen,
To speak and not be heard,
To listen and not understand.

I am inspired by the fact that creativity is limitless, and I should always look for possibilities no matter how far fetched they may seem.

If only for the meanings that
allow pure strains of casualty,
Statistics limited by crowded
commanding knots,
In policies, chains of seductive
cleansers shine this way.

———————●———————

For the purest of forms,
We've been excluded from the revealed future events,
Push pencils and demand,
Site sickens, picked and perceived, here in a corner–
No bigger than what's seen.

Formed in Time

In flesh,
In mind,
Near or far,
The passing of worlds, our souls old and
closer to wisdom will somehow meet again,
To greet passion–
To love forever, each day of new forms,
In your arms–
Beside you.

She was that type–
The color of question, what shade
of blue the sky was that day,
and of course I would smile
with no response,
Birds born to fly away,
Thriving on quick smiles and
even quicker frowns.

To the rest of all,
Who are you?
What's the matter with my sweet chore?
Kiss me green,
Arid grizzly pissing away at stones and starry nights,
My act is honest and pure,
One side commands not over the other
but somewhere in between.

————————●————————

Are my tabs kept?
The eyes in the back of my head are dry and itchy,
Tired–
The visitor was talkative and sometimes revealed–
Walking up the downstairs,
Glossy–
Vibrant–
And new to the mentality of unreason,
Glimpses are caught with no explanation,
only assumption,
It's a place so familiar–
So faint.

Nipples chapped and swollen,
Feet wet and recycled,
Charges applied to a youth,
Born are finances difficult and contained.

———————●———————

auto_matic_8

The creatures in my world do not know of your existence, so why should you know of theirs.

———————•———————

I hear the screams in the night,
Brisk–
Frozen–
Her tattered and abused flesh slammed
doors upon the face of welcome social respects.

———————•———————

Constipated–
Contaminated–
Incubated–
The comments are comprehended,
The response ignored and dissipated.

———————●———————

The episode of lazy existance,
Gestation, awakens repetition of low perception,
Goals stuck in the harboring of safe, stale production.

———————●———————

4 Trees

We do this not for fame or fortune, but out of a
desire to create and share something from within.

Shades of faith, numerous rows from front to back,
Belief was passed never to pause or gasp.

If one takes upon the beliefs of others, then thou are already on the sheep's path.

Expel my ghastly advocate, creator of spells,
Puzzles must determine a master,
The gate will remain.

———•———

auto_matic_09

146 • JOE LOVETT

The art that you feel, is the art that you should create.

———————•———————

The crows come when something dies,
The crows call when someone cries,
Alone–
Remiss.

People fear what they don't understand, and fear
understanding that which is misunderstood even more.

———————•———————

I've defeated all of my friends,
and all of my enemies,
This late night calls no one into question.

———————•———————

Cruel with no hope,
Faint–
The glimpse of nature's beauty,
A child to have never seen the ocean or majestic hills–
Mountains of one's country, dirt roads mired by tyrants,
Minds shallow that dig deep,
sewn in the grave of inhumanity.

————●————

Here we lay–
Sit–
Sprawl–
And adjust in the confines of fabrication,
The influence recognized, hoping not to be noticed.

———————●———————

Sometimes looking at strange things until they become familiar can become a detriment to great insights.

Consumer cathedrals,
Circle of three and only that,
Drooling, closing in on finance,
They were dubbed the vultures of commission.

auto_matic_10

Ninth Step

Cruel pace knocks late, greeted,
Shut behind procedure's ninth step,
we forget not to lock,
Subscribe to our impulse,
stack us neat, with no further use,
Collect corners,
Dank–
Allergic–
Night appears with measurment,
to blind dark pampered eyes.

Making things out to be more than what they are, is
an inherently human condition.

———————●———————

Lost–
A beautiful response to an obsurd question,
Only to recall the duplicate's reduction of integrity.

————•————

Thought–
Beginning–
Process–
Anticipation–
Completion–
Elation–
Depression–
Anticipation–
Thought.

The smooth constraint of industry
farming life to extinction,
We live for the mondain
chastity that entertain portions.

———————•———————

I too am a spectator, a viewer of dreams– I must not deviate.

———————●———————

Remove me–
Blue–
Warm–
Crisp location of dismay.

Graceful Union

When the path of love crosses,
eyes and hearts are opened with infinite devotion,
Now is the time of witness, to share with family,
Friends–
May the light shine upon this graceful union.

auto_matic_19

Enrollment positioned, groomed,
Corners cut, sudden, shallow–
Status blinds standards, open arms create potential
wounds, the taste so sour unable to heal hands,
Destiny's distance came twice.

Brutalities channel broadcast,
soak our conditions, for we must shame our sins,
Plush,
we must construct buttons,
Round,
the dictation of colors must vary.

Exfoliating madness!!!!!!

———————●———————

The face of fear again takes flight,
firm first steps growl at growth's hope,
Ear's naked strain will recognize random placement,
Declared unfit for humane red tape.

———————•———————

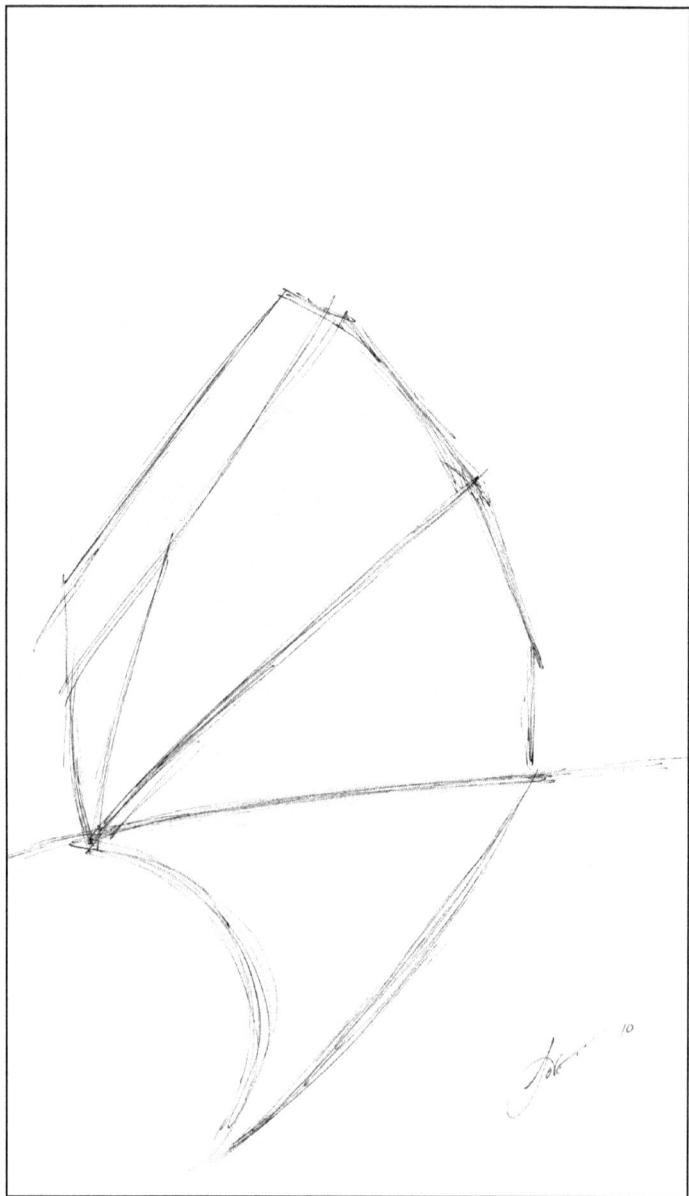

Commonality does not equal compatibility.

————●————

Our nights of procrastination remind us,
scorned by the lack of attention,
disrespect is not the intent,
So I ask not,
But respond to all signals,
I must die and be rebirthed,
The air is thin.

————————●————————

We sell ourselves short with flamboyance.

Allow a temporary time unveiled and rotated,
The chipped tenant should go now before all
clocks reveal closure,
Pockets of glamour and late night opinion
survive plates of left over cuisine.

————————●————————

auto_matic_38

Nervous turbulant youth must not mistake
their questions for knowledge,
Blind–
They face the arrogant fixtures of old.

———————●———————

If you must label it, at least make it original!

———●———

To react to stupidity, only validates the stupid.

As an outsider looking in, I could always see the bull shit coming from a mile away.

———————●———————

With my work, what ifs are unrecognizable, the
end result is execution's identity.

———————●———————

Beauty of the Bird

Graceful blackcock, float on pockets,
Feathers occupy, embraced by wingspans,
Instinct has no question,
No doubt.

Horizontal nosedive will raise the appetite,
crave the plunge attempt to revive,
absence invited, departed,
Civilized and silent, our chain
of command has been pulled,
The consumers packaged
for wide eyed attraction.

———————●———————

The road to self-degradation begins
with the degradation of others.

Burn–
Chop–
Dig–
Bury–
Spill–
Contaminate–
Pollute–
Waste–
Eliminate–
Dictate–
Employ–
Build.

———————●———————

auto_matic_66

Clatter's invoice seemed mature,
Gridlocked–
Wilted evictions invade front lawn episodes,
Camp here for the meager fee of labor.

Hollow heads dissolve quick release tablets
and conquer loud gestures that somehow persist.

———————•———————

Thinking about a small out of the way place, where no one knows my name.

———————●———————

It only takes one person to believe in
something to make it a reality.

———————●———————

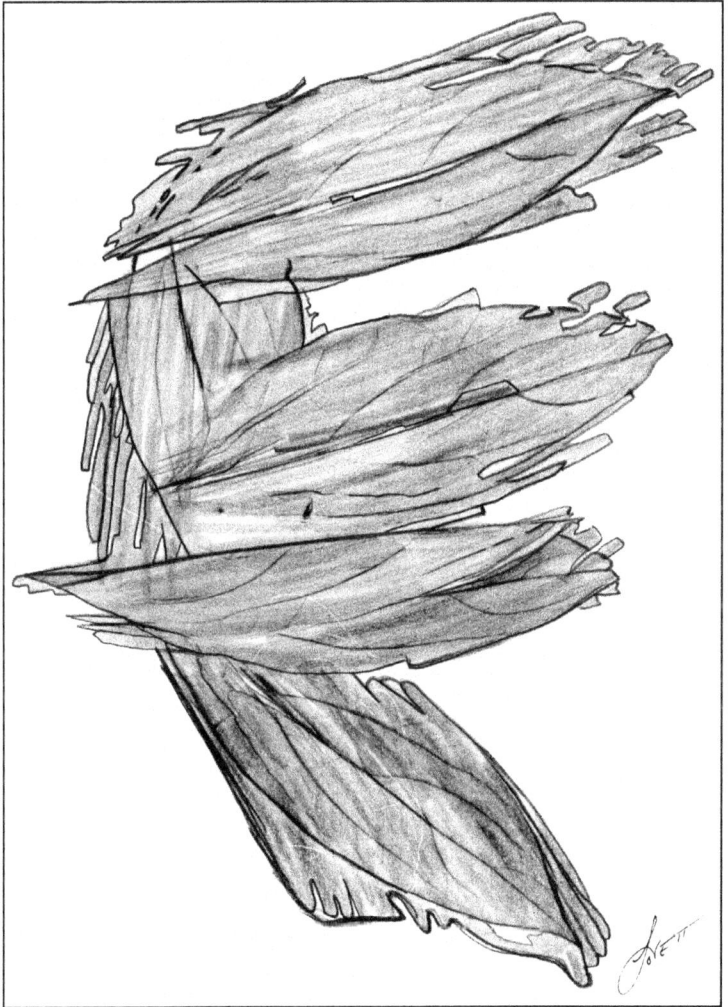

auto_matic_02

My stature is tall, my heart is full, my mind is on everything, my demeanor is reserved, my art is a reflection.

———————•———————

There is no impossible just
possibilities waiting to happen.

———•———

Executing every idea, no matter how ridiculous they may seem.

———————●———————

auto_matic_90

The arrogance of others,
shows me the way of my errs.

————●————

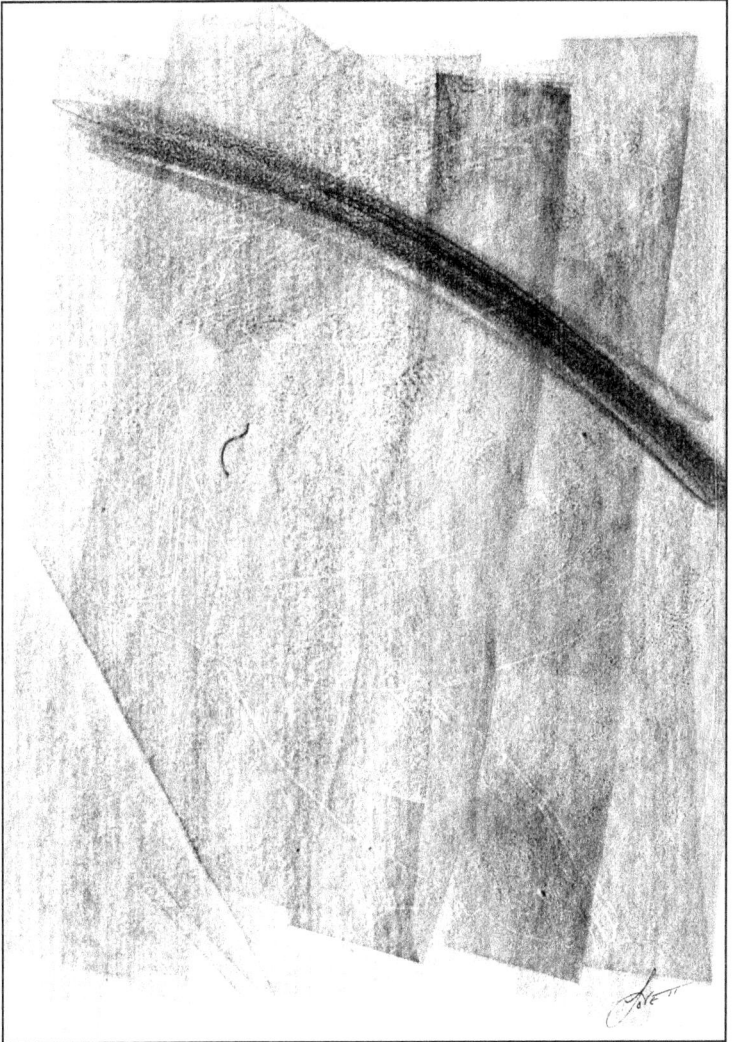

auto_matic_15

As a society, our full potential will never be met, unless we eradicate discrimination.

———————●———————

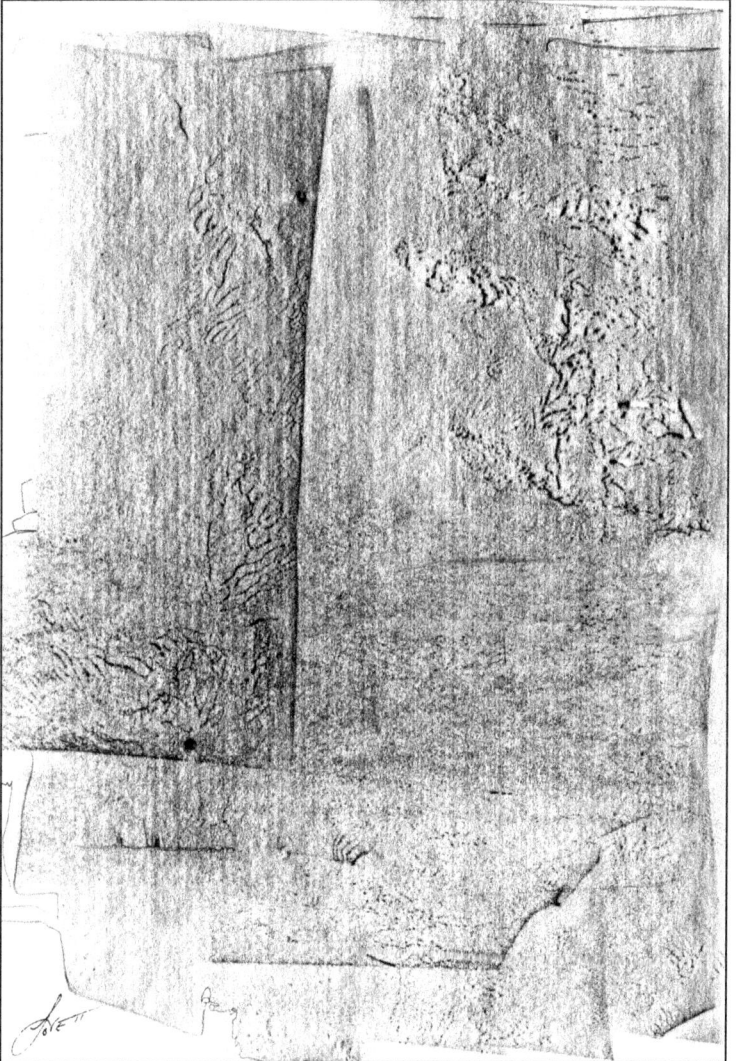

auto_matic_100

Touch of Injury

Dry creation withered,
Old souls have found our grave
in the touch of injury,
Day's long minute on the hour–
A soulless search for audience,
The cast has been made.

I would much rather live a simple
boring life, than a lie.

———————●———————

Public self-deprecation is a cry for invalid reassurance.

————————●————————

Ye who lives in the past never moves forward.

I'm not creating things that resemble everyday life, I am creating things that resemble what I see.

———————●———————

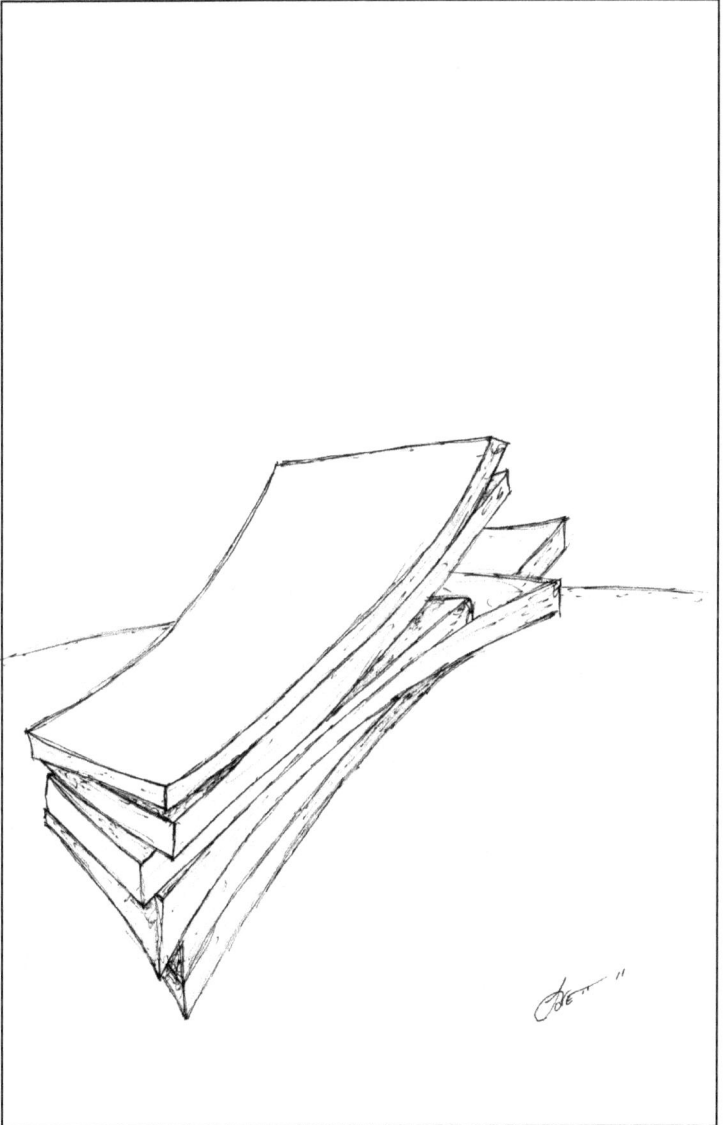

If being accepted means kissing someone's ass, then count me out.

———————●———————

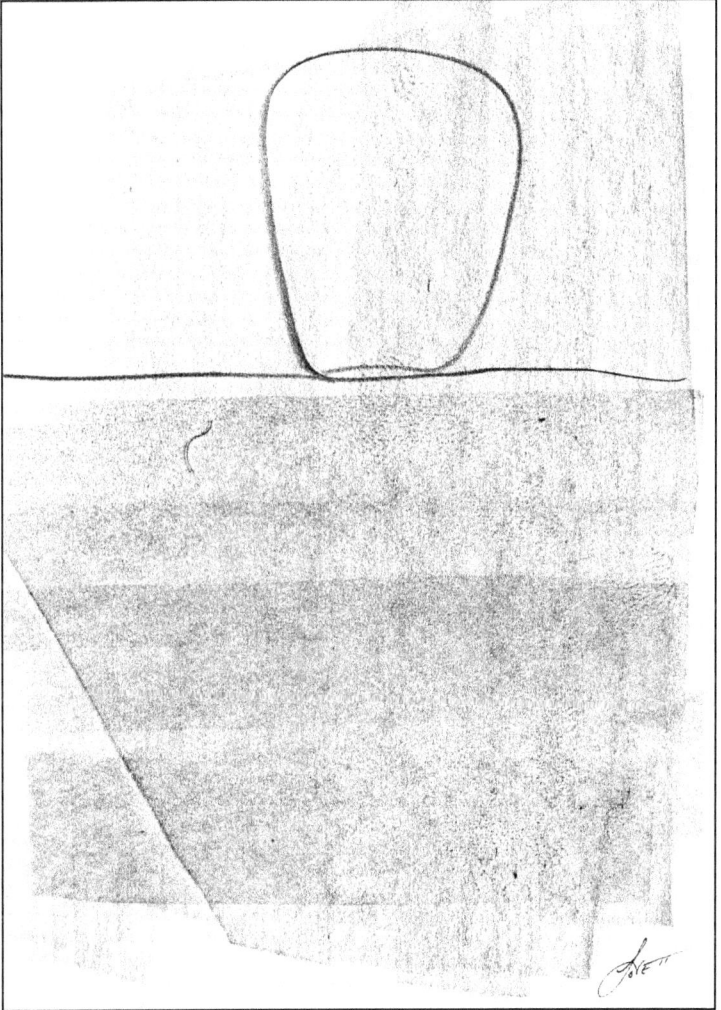

auto_matic_50

Personal victories take time to develop, so do not get discouraged, just know that the goal will soon be complete.

———————●———————

Sometimes you just have to sit and stare endlessly into nowhere.

There's nothing strange about being yourself.

———————•———————

The Crisis

Their bodies shifted with currents of restrictive horror,
The bond was of a strong cast cutting the skin,
Their fate was signed and sealed soon to be delivered,
Blinding darkness bred to cater and build a new nation,
ALL ABOARD–
Your death ship has arrived,
The crisis has begun.

———————•———————

The Crisis

My job is not to entertain the interpretation of the spectator.

If I scare you, that's your problem, don't blame me for your inadequacies.

———————•———————

Someone once asked me if I was trying to take over the world, my response was, just a tiny piece of it.

————————●————————

A tiny yellow man fell from the pocket or the hand,
fell to his mother ground,
Did the child cry long?
Or was it even noticed.

———————•———————

One must first strip away the hometown influence
of limited intentions in order to gain access.

———————•———————

The only mistake that could possibly
be made as a painter is to not paint.

Even the most tarnished of souls has
the potential to become a diamond.

———————●———————

It's easy to find the faults in others, the difficult task is acknowledging your own faults and correcting them.

———●———

A Thought of You

You dominate my dreams of joy,
I smile soft in slumber,
The same holds true,
A memory–
A thought of you.